The NFL's Greatest Teams

DETROIT LIONS

Katie Lajiness

Big Buddy Books
An Imprint of Abdo Publishing
abdopublishing.com

abdopublishing.com

Published by Abdo Publishing, a division of ABDO, PO Box 398166, Minneapolis, Minnesota 55439.

Printed in the United States of America, North Mankato, Minnesota.
092016
012017

THIS BOOK CONTAINS
RECYCLED MATERIALS

Cover Photo: ASSOCIATED PRESS.
Interior Photos: ASSOCIATED PRESS (pp. 5, 7, 9, 11, 13, 15, 17, 18, 19, 20, 21, 22 23, 25, 27, 28, 29); AP (p. 20).

Coordinating Series Editor: Tamara L. Britton
Graphic Design: Michelle Labatt, Taylor Higgins, Jenny Christsensen

Publisher's Cataloging-in-Publication Data

Names: Lajiness, Katie, author.
Title: Detroit Lions / by Katie Lajiness.
Description: Minneapolis, MN : Abdo Publishing, 2017. | Series: NFL's greatest teams | Includes bibliographical references and index.
Identifiers: LCCN 2016944879 | ISBN 9781680785333 (lib. bdg.) | ISBN 9781680798937 (ebook)
Subjects: LCSH: Detroit Lions (Football team)--History--Juvenile literature.
Classification: DDC 796.332--dc23
LC record available at http://lccn.loc.gov/2016944879

Contents

A Winning Team

The Detroit Lions are a football team from Detroit, Michigan. They have played in the National Football League (NFL) for more than 85 years.

The Lions have had good seasons and bad. But time and again, they've proven themselves. Let's see what makes the Lions one of the NFL's greatest teams.

Blue, silver, and white are the team's colors.

PETERSON
10:00

League Play

Team Standings

The NFC and the American Football Conference (AFC) make up the NFL. Each conference has a north, south, east, and west division.

The NFL got its start in 1920. Its teams have changed over the years. Today, there are 32 teams. They make up two conferences and eight divisions.

The Lions play in the North Division of the National Football Conference (NFC). This division also includes the Chicago Bears, the Green Bay Packers, and the Minnesota Vikings.

Fans get excited to watch the Lions play!

The Chicago Bears are a major rival of the Lions. The Bears/Lions rivalry is one of the oldest in NFL history.

Kicking Off

The Lions started out in 1930. In the beginning, the team was based in Ohio. They were known as the Portsmouth Spartans.

In 1934, George A. Richards bought the team. He moved the team to Detroit and changed the name to the Lions. The next year, the Lions won their first NFL **championship**!

In 1932, the Spartans played in the first play-off game in NFL history. They lost to the Chicago Bears 9–0.

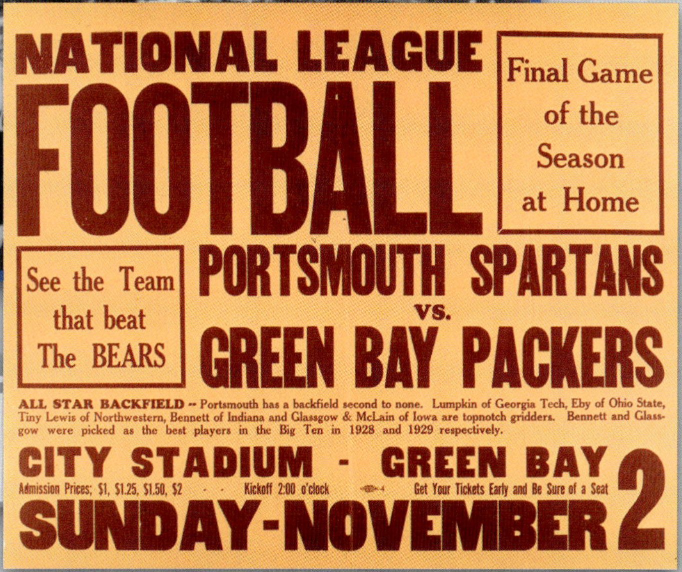

In the 1930s, professional football games were announced on posters.

Highlight Reel

Win or Go Home

NFL teams play 16 regular season games each year. The teams with the best records are part of the play-off games. Play-off winners move on to the conference championships. Then, conference winners face off in the Super Bowl!

During the 1940s, the Lions only had two winning seasons. Then they started to play well again. The team went on to win the NFL **championship** in 1952, 1953, and 1957!

But, the Lions struggled for the next 30 years. The team only made it to the play-offs in 1970 and 1982. Sadly, they lost both times. The Lions finally won their division in 1983. But, again they lost in the play-offs.

Halfback Robert Smith made nine interceptions in 1952. This was the third best in the NFL!

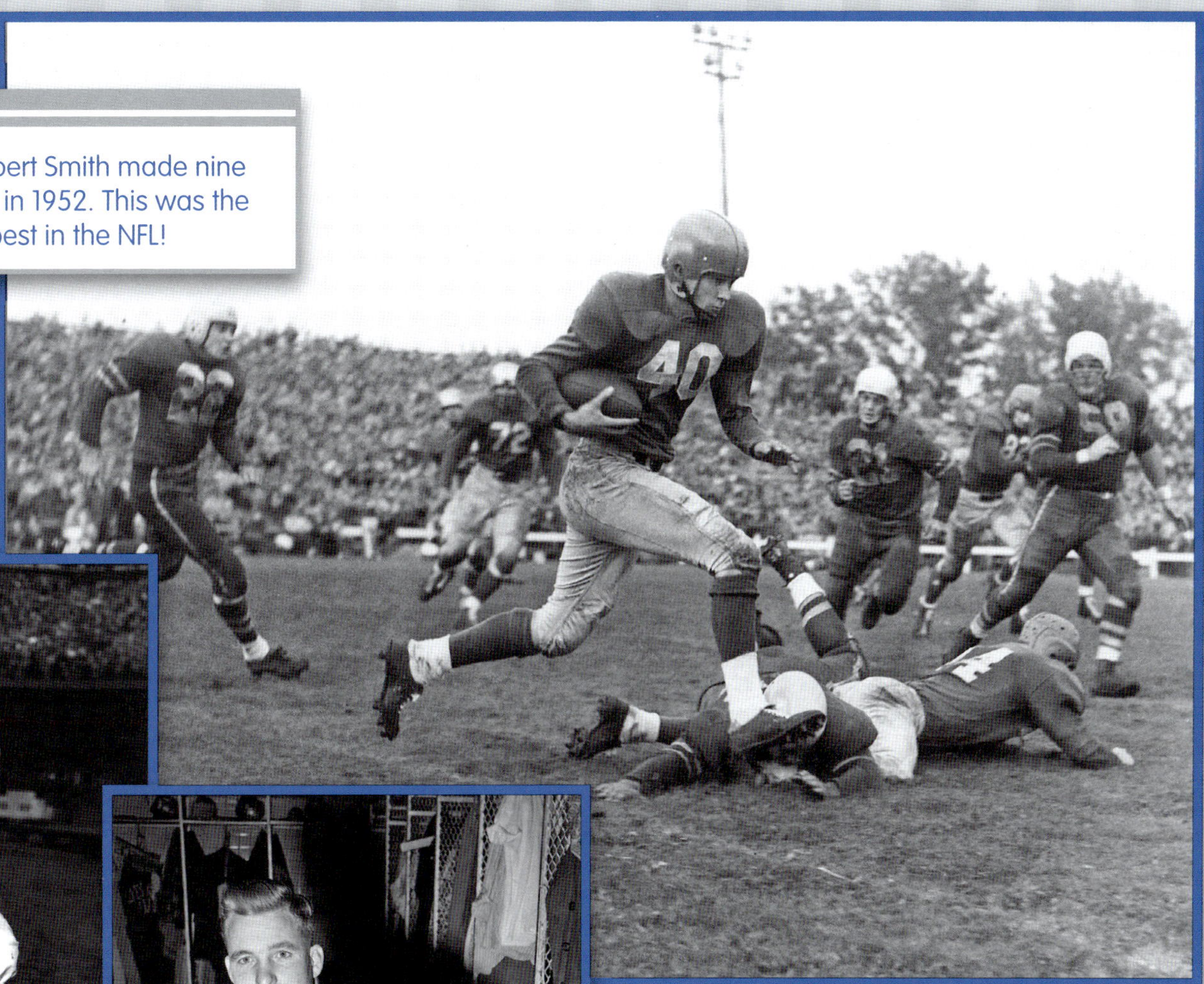

In 1950, star players Doak Walker (left) and Bobby Layne (right) joined the team.

The Lions had better success during the 1990s. Head coach Wayne Fontes and running back Barry Sanders led the team to winning seasons. The Lions won their division in 1991 and 1993. And, they made it to the play-offs six times.

The 2000s were bad years for the Lions. They often were the worst team in their division. And, they never made the play-offs. Today, the Lions are working hard to get back to their former glory.

Barry Sanders holds an NFL record for running 150 yards in 25 games.

Still Waiting

As of 2016, the Lions are one of four NFL teams to never have played in a Super Bowl.

Matthew Stafford made 41 touchdowns in 2011. He holds the team record for most passing touchdowns.

Halftime! Stat Break

Team Records

RUSHING YARDS
Career: Barry Sanders, 15,269 yards (1989–1998)
Single Season: Barry Sanders, 2,053 yards (1997)
PASSING YARDS
Career: Matthew Stafford, 25,976 yards (2009–2015)
Single Season: Matthew Stafford, 5,038 yards (2011)
RECEPTIONS
Career: Calvin Johnson, 731 receptions (2007–2015)
Single Season: Herman Moore, 123 receptions (1995)
ALL-TIME LEADING SCORER
Jason Hanson, 2,150 points (1992–2012)

Championships

EARLY CHAMPIONSHIP WINS:
1935, 1952, 1953, 1957
SUPER BOWL APPEARANCES:
None
SUPER BOWL WINS:
None

Famous Coaches

George Wilson (1957–1964)
Wayne Fontes (1988–1996)

Fan Fun

STADIUM: Ford Field
LOCATION: Detroit, Michigan
MASCOT: Roary
TEAM SONG: "Gridiron Heroes"

Pro Football Hall of Famers & Their Years with the Lions

Lem Barney, Cornerback (1967–1977)
Jack Christiansen, Defensive Back (1951–1958)
Earl "Dutch" Clark, Quarterback (1934–1938)
Lou Creekmur, Tackle/Guard (1950–1959)
Bill Dudley, Halfback (1947–1949)
Dick Lane, Cornerback (1960–1965)
Yale Lary, Defensive Back (1952–1953, 1956–1964)
Bobby Layne, Quarterback (1950–1958)
Dick LeBeau, Cornerback (1959–1972)
Barry Sanders, Running Back (1989–1998)
Charlie Sanders, Tight End (1968–1977)
Joe Schmidt, Linebacker (1953–1965)
Dick Stanfel, Guard (1952–1955)
Doak Walker, Halfback (1950–1955)
Alex Wojciechowicz, Center/Linebacker (1938–1946)

Coaches' Corner

In 1957, George Wilson became the Lions head coach. That year, the team won the NFL **championship**. Wilson was the first coach to win the NFL Coach of the Year **award**.

Coach Wayne Fontes joined the team in 1988. He led the Lions to the play-offs four times. Fontes was named NFL Coach of the Year in 1991.

Fontes coached the Lions to a 12–4 season in 1991. This was the most successsful season in the team's history.

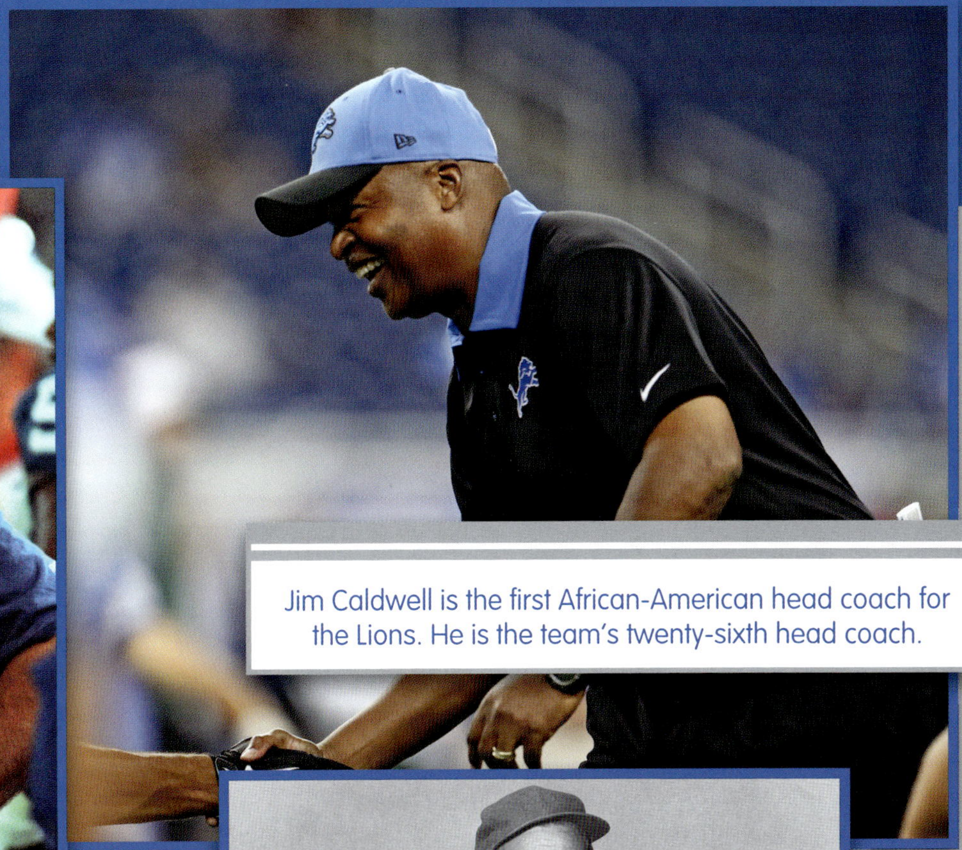

Jim Caldwell is the first African-American head coach for the Lions. He is the team's twenty-sixth head coach.

In 1957, Wilson led the Lions to a 59–14 win over the Cleveland Browns.

Star Players

Earl "Dutch" Clark

QUARTERBACK
(1934–1938)

Earl "Dutch" Clark was one of the original Lions players. Clark led the league in scoring three times during his **career**. He even kicked field goals and extra points. Clark became the first member of the Lions to join the Pro Football Hall of Fame.

Doak Walker HALFBACK (1950–1955)

When Doak Walker joined the team in 1950, many people thought he was too small to play in the NFL. But, he proved them wrong. In his first year, Walker was named **Rookie** of the Year. He was a key player during the team's glory years. During his six-year **career** with the Lions, Walker scored 534 points.

Bobby Layne QUARTERBACK (1950–1958)

The Lions got Bobby Layne in a trade in 1950. Layne led the Lions to three NFL **championships**. In 1956, he was also the best kicker in the NFL! Layne became the lead kicker for the 1956 and 1957 seasons.

Dick Lane CORNERBACK (1960–1965)

Dick Lane played six seasons with the Lions. During that time, Lane had 21 **interceptions** for 272 yards and one touchdown. He was named to the Pro Bowl, which is the NFL's all-star game, three times. In 1974, Lane joined the Pro Football Hall of Fame.

Barry Sanders RUNNING BACK (1989–1998)

Barry Sanders was one of the best running backs in NFL history. He was named **Rookie** of the Year in 1989 and Most Valuable Player (MVP) in 1997. Sanders was the first running back to rush for more than 1,000 yards in ten straight seasons. In 2004, he joined the Pro Football Hall of Fame.

Calvin Johnson WIDE RECEIVER (2007–2015)

In 2007, Calvin Johnson was the second player the Lions picked. In 2012, Johnson set an NFL record with 1,964 receiving yards! He set another record with 100 receiving yards in eight back-to-back games. Johnson played his entire **career** with the Lions.

Matthew Stafford QUARTERBACK (2009–)

Matthew Stafford was the first Lions **rookie** quarterback to start a season since 1968. He became the youngest quarterback to throw five or more touchdowns in a single game. In 2015, Stafford became the fastest player in NFL history to reach 25,000 passing yards. Stafford also holds many of the team's passing records.

Ford Field

The Lions play home games at Ford Field. It is in Detroit. Ford Field opened in 2002. It holds 65,000 people.

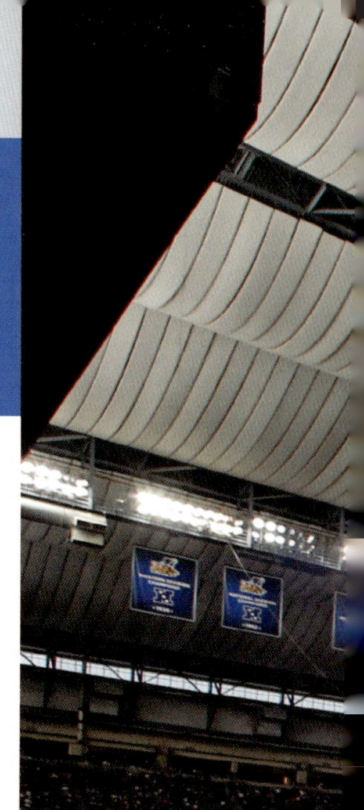

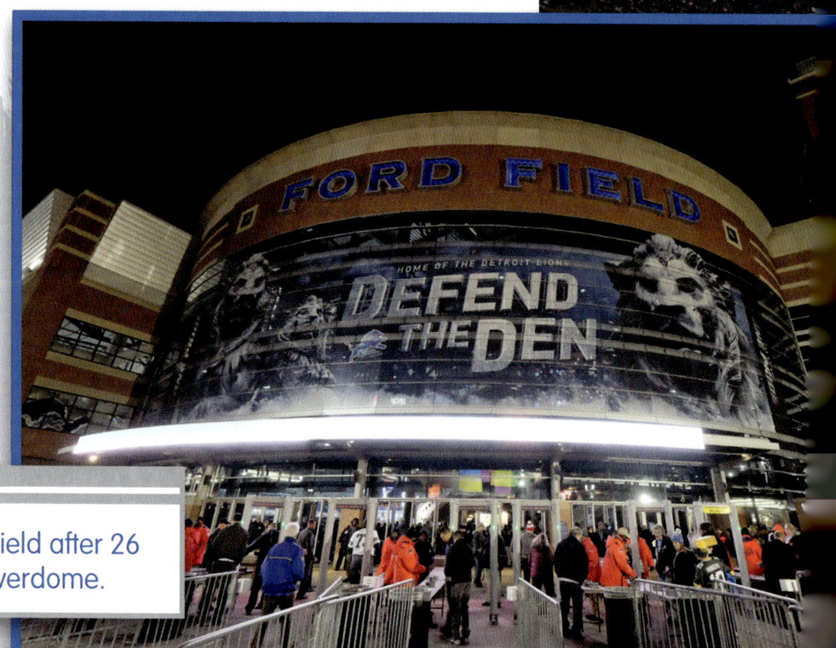

The Lions moved to Ford Field after 26 years at the Pontiac Silverdome.

Ford Field hosted the 2006 Super Bowl.

Go Lions!

Thousands of fans flock to Ford Field to see the Lions play home games. The team's **mascot** is Roary. He helps fans cheer on the Lions at home games.

Lions fans are very faithful to the team. In 1934, the team played its first game on Thanksgiving day. Today, thousands of fans still attend the team's Thanksgiving day game.

The Lions played the Chicago Bears in the first Thanksgiving-day game. About 26,000 fans came to watch.

Roary also visits kids at elementary schools. He teaches leadership skills.

Fans love to watch the Lions play!

Final Call

The Lions have a long, rich history. They won four early NFL **championships**.

Even during losing seasons, true fans have stuck by them. Many believe the Detroit Lions will remain one of the greatest teams in the NFL.

In 2011, Dominic Raiola (left) and Stephen Peterman (right) hugged after an 88-yard touchdown!

Through the Years

1934

The Lions play their first game in Detroit.

1935

The Lions play the New York Giants in the first NFL **championship**. They win 26–7!

1957

The Lions play the Cleveland Browns in the NFL championship. The Lions win for the fourth time.

1992

The Lions beat the Dallas Cowboys 38–6 in the play-offs. This is the team's first play-off win since 1957.

1999

Popular running back Barry Sanders **retires** from football.

2008

The Lions are winless with a 0–16 record for the season.

2009

The team has the first pick in the NFL **draft**. They choose quarterback Matt Stafford.

2011

The Lions earn their first play-off appearance in 12 years.

Postgame Recap

1. What is the name of the stadium where the Lions play home games?
   A. Ford Field **B**. Scion Stadium **C**. Dodge Dome

2. Name 3 of the 15 Lions in the Pro Football Hall of Fame.

3. What year did the team move to Detroit?
   A. 1954
   B. 1944
   C. 1934

4. What is the name of the team's mascot?
   A. Simba
   B. Roary
   C. Prowler

1. A. 2. See page 15. 3. C. 4. B.

Glossary

award something that is given in recognition of good work or a good act.

career a period of time spent in a certain job.

championship a game, a match, or a race held to find a first-place winner.

draft a system for professional sports teams to choose new players.

interception (ihn-tuhr-SEHP-shuhn) when a player catches a pass that was meant for the other team's player.

mascot something to bring good luck and help cheer on a team.

retire to give up one's job.

rookie a first-year player in a professional sport.

Websites

To learn more about the NFL's Greatest Teams, visit **booklinks.abdopublishing.com**. These links are routinely monitored and updated to provide the most current information available.

Index

INSECTOS EN TU JARDÍN

VEO HORMIGAS

por Genevieve Nilsen

TABLA DE CONTENIDO

tadpole en español

VEO HORMIGAS

Veo hormigas.

Son pequeñas.

Veo hormigas.

Caminan en fila.

Veo hormigas.

Comen.

Veo hormigas.

Beben.

Veo hormigas.

Levantan.

Veo hormigas.

Suben.

Veo hormigas.

Trabajan juntas.

REPASO DE PALABRAS

beben

caminan

comen

levantan

suben

trabajan

ÍNDICE